# POTENTIAL PARTNERS IN THE PACIFIC? SOFT POWER AND THE SINO-NATO RELATIONSHIP

We don't want to compete with the United Nations. We don't want to turn NATO into a global security agency. The aim must be that the transatlantic partnership is complemented in a very natural way by the trans-Pacific partnership. We need an answer as to how we shape the alliance's relationship with China.[1]

– Former German Defense Minister Karl-Theodor zu Guttenberg

Recently, China's soft power engagements have increased in both frequency and scope, leading many observers to speculate about future possibilities for these types of activities.[2] At the same time, the North Atlantic Treaty Alliance (NATO) has adopted a new Strategic Concept which calls for "dialogue and cooperation" and a "wide network of partner relationships with countries and organisations around the globe"[3] – verbiage that has undertones of exerting influence through persuasion, the hallmark of soft power.[4] Is there mutual benefit in a relationship between China and NATO? What shape might such a relationship take, and what are the ramifications for both China and NATO member states? This paper will argue that NATO and China share a common interest in maintaining security of the "global commons'" those public goods over which no state has a generally recognized exclusive jurisdiction,[5] but which can offer benefits to all countries in the international community. Such dialogue with the Chinese offers the potential to enhance the Alliance's ability to extend cooperative security beyond the Euro-Atlantic area, and it offers the Chinese a means for protecting their interests on the global stage in a constructive, non-threatening manner that is also in line with their "lay low" (Tao Guang Yang Hui) foreign policy.

---

[*] The views expressed in this paper are those of the author. They do not necessarily reflect the official policy or position of the Department of Defense, the U.S. Army, or the United States Military Academy at West Point.

1

At first glance, China and the North Atlantic Treaty Alliance (NATO) appear to have little to offer one another. Under the leadership of President Hu Jintao, China insists that it seeks "peaceful development" and firmly eschews alliances, while NATO – an established military alliance – currently has a full agenda dealing with current members, potential future members, and former enemies. NATO is also deeply involved in an out-of-area mission in Afghanistan, a situation that dominates the Alliance's time, attention, and resources – as well as coloring much of the Alliance's interaction with non-member nations.[6] China is also interested in Afghanistan, for both strategic and economic purposes: the two countries share a short 76 kilometer (about 47.2 mile) border (over which destabilizing forces such as drugs and terrorists could potentially flow), and the mineral wealth hidden in Afghanistan has attracted China's attention. Indeed, the 2007 announcement that the Chinese Metallurgical Corporation had won the rights to develop the Anyak Copper Mine just south of Kabul made global headlines, leaving many analysts to speculate on China's intentions and the implications for the future of Afghanistan.[7] Yet for many reasons, Afghanistan does not offer the most fertile common ground for long-term relationship-building between NATO and China. Instead, mutual functional interests in soft power pursuits such as crisis management, humanitarian assistance/disaster relief (HA/DR), nonproliferation, and globally-sanctioned operations which protect common goods (such as counter-piracy operations) will serve as the critical interests which have the potential to drive the relationship forward.

The path ahead for Sino-NATO cooperation is full of potential pitfalls, and is by no means clear. However, if successfully navigated, it could result in the development of a NATO-China relationship and a more secure global situation through the engagement of an increasingly powerful China with an established organization dedicated to ensuring stability and security. The onus for moving forward is clearly on NATO: China does not need to interact with the Alliance. Beijing has other, preferred options for global engagement in the security realm, on bi-lateral, regional (European Union, Shanghai Cooperation Organization) and global (United Nations) bases. So the challenge to NATO is clear: how can the Alliance convince China to develop a relationship?

Perhaps a better question is one of intent: why should NATO entice China to interact? NATO's current Secretary General, Anders Fogh Rasmussen, has provided a possible answer: transforming the Alliance into a global role would allow NATO to more effectively counter threats which increasingly come from far beyond the Alliance's borders such as terrorism, piracy, energy cut-offs, and climate change[8] This transformation is a key objective of NATO's Strategic Concept and one that the Secretary General has personally embraced. Rasmussen is actively pursuing relationships with Brazil, India, and China as he tries to put NATO in a more global stance.[9] Transformation of the Alliance would also allow NATO to counter lingering, persistent questions of relevancy in a post-Soviet (and eventually, after 2014, a post-ISAF) world.

An underlying assumption of this study, and one clearly indicated by both parties, is that any interaction between NATO and China will develop from the intersection of interests. Understanding the interests of each side is challenging as there are many internal and domestic components from which state and institutional interests are derived, which calls into question the unitary actor assumption. This is particularly true in the case of an alliance such as NATO which has 28 member nations, each with their own domestic political considerations. Recognizing this limitation inherent in discerning intent, this paper will take stated interests at face value, use them to help explain the past Sino-NATO relationship, and to provide a framework for understanding the potential for future interaction.

## A CHECKERED PAST – COLD WAR INDEFFERENCE TO INTEREST

During the Cold War, while China's relationship with NATO was virtually non-existent, international actions taken by either party had effects on policies enacted by the other. During the early years of the Alliance there was little cause to interact with China, an Asian country concerned with defining and preserving its own territorial integrity which had expressed no desire for involvement on the European continent. China's focus was on territorial consolidation and recovery after almost two decades of war, while NATO's Charter concentrated on establishing a collective defense alliance against the Soviet Union and its allies. Meanwhile, China entered into the Sino-Soviet Treaty of Friendship, Alliance, and Mutual Assistance (formally signed on 14 February 1950) effectively allying Beijing with Moscow.[10] This treaty "specified the duty of mutual assistance in the case of aggression by a third country, the duties not to participate in any alliance or coalition against the other, and the obligation to consult with each other on all important international issues concerning common interests."[11] In theory, this made NATO a common enemy, although little documentation exists to provide insight into Chinese thoughts on the Alliance during this time. Initially, Chairman Mao advocated deliberately maintaining an aloofness from the Western-bloc countries, consistent with the guiding principles of Chinese foreign policy at the time[12] which emphasized cohesiveness with fellow Socialist states and development of internal cohesion and strength to counter any possible Western influence. This was the famous "lean to one side" policy that Mao articulated on 30 June 1949, placing the PRC firmly on the side of socialism and against imperialism, identified with the capitalistic West.[13]

The role of the United States in the Alliance also caused concern, and there is evidence of negative Chinese feelings toward this special transatlantic security relationship. As retired PLA Major General Pan Zhenqiang (current Professor at the Institute of Strategic Studies at the National Defense University, PLA, China) writes, "In the Cold War, China was opposed to the US using NATO as a tool for the purpose of controlling Europe and intensifying competition with the Soviet Union for global

3

supremacy."[14]  In China's view, the Alliance served as a means of projecting US power on the European continent – power directed against the USSR, which was Beijing's ally at the time.

NATO's focus was on the containment of the USSR and, by proxy, world socialism; and thus China had a reason to distrust the Alliance.  Xinghui Zhang, a journalist for a major Chinese newspaper, wrote in 2009 about what NATO meant to him:

> It was an operationally mysterious, geographically faraway and adversarial organisation. This held true during the Cold War - and in certain periods after.
>
> Why? Well, it was 'operationally mysterious' mainly because of its opaque policy-making process and the fact that its activities had little to do with Chinese political, economic or social life. It was 'geographically faraway', because all its members are Western European and Northern American countries. And it was 'adversarial' because its original core purpose was to confront the former Soviet Union Communist Bloc.
>
> For these reasons, I once viewed NATO as a 'big stranger' and considered it a tool used by the USA to expand its 'global hegemony.'[15]

The outbreak of the Korean War in June 1950 further alienated the Chinese from those countries supporting the UN-sanctioned defense of South Korea, many of which were NATO members.  Although the Alliance itself did not participate in the conflict, NATO member states provided troops and aid to the United Nations Command (Korea),[16] and the conflict had the effect of raising the perceived communist threat level and thus compelling the alliance to develop concrete strategic and military plans.[17]  This directly led to the establishment of an integrated military force under centralized command, and to the creation of the position of Supreme Allied Commander, Europe (SACEUR) in late 1950 and the Supreme Headquarters, Allied Forces, Europe (SHAPE) in early 1951.[18]  Chinese support of North Korea during the war solidified Alliance concerns regarding the Communist threat, and many within NATO saw this conflict as a small proxy for what could occur between Western Europe and the Soviet Union.[19]

The 1960s brought the Sino-Soviet split and Chinese foreign policy became increasingly isolated and nationalistic.  NATO, never prominent on China's list of priorities, now became even less so.  Yet it would be misleading to suggest that the status quo dominated; China did appreciate the pressure that NATO placed on the USSR; it served as a useful means of counterbalancing and potentially weakening her former ally.  From Beijing's standpoint, the interests that dominated during this time of the after-effects of the Great Leap Forward and the throes of the Cultural Revolution were internal ones, designed to maintain national unity (even in the face of high-level internal power plays) and secure China's borders.

After China normalized relations with the United States in 1972, there is some evidence that the American leadership tried to convince Beijing that the Soviets were more of a threat to Chinese, rather than NATO, interests.  For example, this excerpt from Henry Kissinger's August 4, 1972 conversation with Huang Hua, the Chinese Ambassador to the United Nations indicates Kissinger's attempt to persuade the PRC that Moscow threatened Chinese interests:

> Our analysis is that there is a deliberate Soviet policy to isolate you, and that the many agreements the Soviet Union has made in the last two years and the patience they have shown in the face of setbacks in the West, can only be explained to us in terms of aggressive intent in the East…This is our analysis. (…) We believe also that it is against our interests to permit the establishment of hegemony in Eurasia dominated from Moscow.[20]

There is evidence that the Chinese disputed Kissinger's representations of Soviet strategy; and Huang's response to Kissinger was that Beijing "was not so worried about the Soviet attempt to isolate China."[21]

Yet China's perception of her interests in the aftermath of normalization appeared to recognize the benefits of Western powers maintaining a counter to Soviet pressures internationally.[22] Mao asserted that the United States and China should cooperate in dealing with the Soviet "bastard" and urged Washington to work more closely with its allies, particularly to maintain NATO unity.[23] In this way, NATO served a useful purpose to Beijing: it created pressure on the USSR, which forced the Soviets to dedicate time and resources in response – resources which Moscow could then not focus on countering China.

## THE COLD WAR ENDS, NATO ENDURES: OPERATIONS IN THE BALKANS AND UNEXPECTED EFFECTS

In the aftermath of the dissolution of the Soviet Union, some Chinese observers believed that the NATO alliance was a relic of the Cold War, and thus should soon disband. As China's former ambassador to the European Union, Ding Yuanhong, noted, "…the basis of the US-European alliance is nonexistent with the Soviet disintegration, dramatic changes in Eastern Europe, and the declining power of Russia."[24] The expansion of the Alliance eastward also alarmed the Chinese. The People's Daily reported in an article entitled "Basic facts about NATO," that "NATO's enlargement is considered a way essentially to serve U.S.'s goal of dominating the world by continuing its control in Europe."[25]

Recognizing the preeminence of the transatlantic connection within the Alliance, and preferring to counter US influence through a multipolar approach, China also sought to deepen ties with the European Union. Official relations between the European Union and China first developed in 1975 and are now governed by the 1985 EU-China Trade and Cooperation Agreement.[26] China consistently sought to emphasize the notion that the presence of the United States in NATO served to prevent Europe from reaching its independent international potential, and hence Beijing preferred to interact with Europe via the European Union. The European Union's predominantly economic focus appealed to the Chinese, whose own economy liberalized during the 1980s under the reform of Deng Xiaoping, and Beijing took a very pragmatic approach to relations with one of its largest trading partners.[27]

Yet all was not smooth in Sino-EU relations; prior to the dissolution of the Soviet Union, the European Union reacted to the 1989 Chinese Communist Party's use of the PLA to violently suppress demonstrations in Tiananmen Square by enacting an arms embargo. In late June 1989, the Council of Ministers issued a Declaration on China stating that it adopted an "interruption by the member states of the community of military cooperation and an embargo on trade in arms with China."[28] The absence of further guidance on what exactly constituted "arms" left the decision up to individual member states to interpret the embargo in the context of "their national laws, regulations, and decision-making processes."[29] This arms embargo, which continues today, has been a source of tension in the Sino-EU relationship and the Chinese continue to press EU members, both collectively and bi-laterally, to remove the restrictions and permit Beijing to purchase weaponry.

Beijing's relations with NATO experienced an unexpected crisis with the 1999 NATO bombing of the Chinese Embassy in Belgrade, Serbia. On 7 May 1999 US bombers, flying as part of the NATO bombing campaign, fired five laser-guided bombs into the Chinese Embassy, killing three and wounding 27 Embassy employees.[30]

The Chinese reaction was swift and angry: protests erupted across the country, directed against Western embassies and consulates, particularly those of the United States and Great Britain, as large crowds threw "eggs, stones, paint balloons, and chunks of concrete" at these buildings, damaging them and trapping Embassy employees inside.[31] The Chinese government immediately condemned the bombing by "the US-led NATO;" suspended military-to-military relations with the United States; postponed China-US consultations on non-proliferation, arms control and international security; and suspended dialogue on human rights.[32] The United States compensated Beijing for both the loss of life and damage to the Embassy building.[33]

Upon the 10th anniversary of the bombings, in 2009, the People's Daily published an article commemorating the event, and the language used indicates that the Chinese do not accept the official NATO explanation of the bombing as a tragic mistake:

> On the night of May 7, 1999, local time for Belgrade, (the early morning of May 8 in Beijing), the North Atlantic Treaty Organization (NATO), headed by the US, brazenly used missiles to attack China's embassy in Belgrade, leading to the death of three Chinese reporters and severe damage of embassy houses. This was a barbaric scene in human history.
>
> Ten years later, US media has selectively forgotten this event, and re-examinations by US authorities are rare. "Mistaken Bombing" is the final explanation and attitude of the US.
>
> A member of the US president China-focused advisory group said that China has already risen 10 years after the event, and the relations between China and the US have been stable and developed a good momentum. The "Mistaken Bombing" has become a blip in history. Experts on China's military issues believe however, that over the past 10 years, it

is just because China has made such tremendous and sincere efforts that the cooperation between China and the US has expanded rather than stagnated.[34]

The verbiage makes it clear that while this may have been a NATO operation, Beijing holds the United States responsible for the event. This blurring of distinction between NATO and the United States works to the detriment of a Chinese relationship with NATO; if Beijing does not view the Alliance as a separate, independent entity, but rather a proxy of the United States, then it becomes difficult to foresee future cooperation or partnership. Why partner with NATO when China can just deal more directly, and bi-laterally, with the United States? If NATO cannot provide a convincing answer to this question, and a means of articulating the distinction to the Chinese, developing and deepening a relationship with Beijing could prove difficult.

The ferocity of the anti-NATO sentiment related to the bombing lingers among Chinese citizens, even in 2011. Chinese graduate students studying at the Ash Center at Harvard's John F. Kennedy School of Government admitted that they (and ordinary Chinese) do not think about NATO much, but when they do, as one student elaborated, "the only memory of NATO for me" was the bombing of 1999.[35] Yao Yao, a member of China's Ministry of Foreign Affairs who worked for the PRC Ambassador to the United States in 1999, said that the bombing made all Chinese "very angry. Most Chinese leaders do not believe in these mistakes because the US has powerful and accurate machines."[36] Yao elaborated that these 1999 events created many negative grassroots feelings among the Chinese toward the United States and NATO. This grassroots resistance may present an obstacle to future Sino-NATO cooperation, and would require Chinese government engagement to overcome with explanations and rationales for a closer relationship with NATO. This is a "cost" for the Chinese government to consider and it may very well prove one that is not palatable for China to undertake, particularly if expanded relations with NATO continue to hold a low priority.

At the official level, the Chinese have not raised the bombing with NATO representatives, indicating that it will not serve as an impediment to further dialogue.[37] This provides evidence that Chinese policymakers are pragmatic when it comes to engagement with NATO, and thus perhaps see some benefits they can gain through interaction. As a US official working Asian Affairs noted, association with NATO provides a means for the Chinese to gain access to and insights on military operations, and to better understand the strengths and weaknesses of allied operations.[38] The Chinese stand to gain valuable insights, and this may provide reason enough for Beijing to keep the door of potential cooperation open.

## NATO IN THE NEIGHBORHOOD: AFGHANISTAN PROPELS THE RELATIONSHIP

In the aftermath of the 9/11 attacks on the Pentagon and the World Trade Center in the United States, NATO invoked the collective defense provisions of Article 5 and, with the December 2001 Bonn

Agreement, requested the United Nations to authorize the development of a security force to assist in maintaining security in Kabul and its surrounding areas.[39] On 20 December 2001 the International Security Assistance Force (ISAF), sanctioned by the UN Security Council (UNSCR 1386), came into existence, marking NATO's formal commitment to providing assistance in three areas: 1) developing national security structures, 2) reconstruction and 3) developing and training future Afghan security forces.[40] NATO was now involved in a country directly bordering China, but, in contrast to the position taken after the 1979 Soviet invasion of Afghanistan, in 2002 Beijing cautiously supported the intervention, and utilized its position on the UN Security Council to support Resolution 1368 creating ISAF. Notably, this was the "first time that China has voted in favor of authorizing the international use of force."[41] President Jiang Zemin was one of the first world leaders to call President Bush and express condolences and outrage at the attack.[42] But as J. Mohan Malik notes, "some Chinese intellectuals and officials reacted gleefully to the attacks," but "Chinese authorities quickly cracked down on celebrations and rejoicing among some of their citizens and in Internet chat rooms."[43]

China's support for the mission in Afghanistan evolved out of Beijing's interest in suppressing Islamic extremists operating in the Xinjiang Autonomous Region – particularly the East Turkestan Islamic Party (ETIP) and the East Turkestan Liberation Organization (or Sharki Turkestan Azatlik Tashkilati (SHAT)).[44] In the wake of the September 11th attacks, Beijing pressured the United States to recognize these groups as terrorist organizations, while human rights organizations saw this as an attempt to allow the government to persecute ethnic Uighur dissent or calls for true autonomy and self-determination in Xinjiang. In August 2002, the US State Department listed the ETIM as a terrorist organization, and the United Nations followed suit on 12 September 2002.[45] China received what it sought: the international backing and legitimatization of its own fight on terrorism. Since Beijing received this positive reinforcement, the Chinese government may be more inclined to assess cooperation in trans-national issues such as terrorism, if properly managed, as a means to an end, with resulting benefits directly related to core national interests.[46]

So, in 2002 - just three years after the Embassy bombing in Belgrade - the Chinese government initiated a relationship with NATO, indicating that at the official governmental level, the incident in Belgrade did not present an impediment to further dialogue. Zuqian Zhang, the director of European Studies at the Shanghai Institute for International Studies, wrote in the autumn of 2003 that the Chinese ambassador to Brussels had met with NATO Secretary General Lord Robertson "to discuss the potential for building a closer relationship between his country and the Alliance."[47] Zuqian attributes this initial contact to the then-recent Chinese integration into the WTO, noting that it would be "only a matter of time" before China also integrated itself into the international security system.[48] Of course, Zuqian acknowledges that NATO's assumption of ISAF's mission in Afghanistan also played a role in the timing of Chinese contact with NATO. From this, we can discern two potential interests: a Chinese place in the international community commensurate with her status, and an acknowledgement that ISAF was operating within the borders of a neighbor, which warranted attention.

From NATO's perspective, China's continued support of the ISAF mission is necessary to maintain the legitimacy of the operation. As a European source commented, ISAF is operating in Afghanistan due to a United Nations mandate, so China's seat on the Security Council provides a necessary vote to secure the continuation of this international authorization.[49] China's relevance to the regional strategic picture is also of interest to NATO, particularly given Beijing's ties to and support of Pakistan. China has been a steadfast ally to Islamabad over the past several decades, supporting both its conventional and nuclear weapons programs, and the influence that Beijing has in Pakistan is considerable.[50] NATO could also benefit from an enlarged Chinese role in Afghanistan for "burden sharing" reasons: perceptions exist that Beijing is freeloading, reaping economic benefits through investment in natural resources while not shouldering much of the security burden. Some Western commentators, such as Anne Applebaum, have decried this NATO willingness to shed blood and spend treasure to secure China's ability to mine natural resources, articulating the concern that this will serve to strengthen China at the expense of Western powers.[51] Other scholars have countered that this is a short-term view, and that in fact, Chinese investment in Afghanistan holds great hope for long-term stabilization of the region.[52] But both sides implicitly agree that Chinese involvement in Afghanistan holds the potential to assist NATO's stabilization mission through contributing necessary resourcing.

From Beijing's perspective, the large role that the United States plays in the Afghanistan endeavor is quite clear, and thus China warily eyes all moves for signs that may lead to an increase in American power or influence in the region. As the Hudson Institute's Richard Weitz recently argued, the paradoxes and contradictions that pervade China's policies towards Afghanistan (such as a desire for security in the region, but opposition of a long-term Western military presence in the area) will make it "extremely difficult" for the United States to establish a strategic partnership with China in Afghanistan.[53] And Roger Cliff indicated in testimony before the US – China Economic and Security Review Commission:

> Given Beijing's fundamental mistrust of US objectives, Beijing will view most, if not all, US regional security initiatives through a "containment" lens. I believe that there is little that US policy makers can do to change this in the short term. Over time, however, welcoming increased Chinese involvement in, and capabilities for, non-combat humanitarian, disaster relief, and peacekeeping operations both in and beyond Asia will provide a means for building mutual confidence.[54]

But will this mistrust of US motives also stymie NATO's ability to build a partnership with China centered on ensuring a secure Afghanistan? It has seemed to limit Beijing's response to overtures by NATO, and China currently does not "partner" with NATO in any official capacity as Japan does. The

PLA has maintained its distance from engaging in any high-level dialogue with NATO, preferring instead to have the Ministry of Foreign Affairs (MFA) conduct policy discussions, which limits the "buy-in" that the military experiences from these efforts.[55] Indeed, some US officials believe that the ISAF coalition is currently "getting all that we can" from China with regards to Afghanistan, because Beijing is not being obstructionist.[56]

Despite this, some encouraging signs do exist. For example, a product of NATO Deputy Secretary General's 2009 visit to Beijing was an offer by the Chinese MFA to develop contacts with NATO in Afghanistan. The Chinese Ambassador in Afghanistan has held periodic meetings with the Senior Civilian Representative (SCR) to ISAF to dialogue regarding matters related to the safety of Chinese workers in the country.[57] This concern over security related to economic/business interests may signal a growing trend in Chinese international involvement; Beijing's businessman are operating in some globally dangerous areas, and ensuring their security may serve to steer Chinese policies in directions which lead to increased interaction with international security organizations such as NATO. It also provides clear evidence of Chinese willingness to engage in dialogue when Beijing deems its interests would benefit.

While Afghanistan does provide a venue for some Sino-NATO coordination, it does not offer the best potential for a long-term relationship; the mutual interests are simply not compelling enough to overcome mutual concerns about cooperation there. However, signs do exist which indicate that NATO's relevance to China may be its identity as an international security alliance – and one that Beijing recognizes as containing some possibilities for interaction through protection of the global commons.

## TESTING THE WATERS – THE GLOBAL COMMONS AS A MUTUAL INTEREST

China's thirst for resources to fuel her 10% per year growth rate has led to a close interest in maintaining the sea lines of communication that allow unfettered access to these goods. So some of Beijing's first ventures in the international security arena have dealt with maritime security, specifically countering piracy. China currently has three ships patrolling the Gulf of Aden and participates in Shared Awareness and Deconfliction (SHADE), a group that ensures communication between the many ships and navies now protecting shipping off the Horn of Africa.[58]

Initial involvement with NATO also involved maritime activities, and Beijing reinforced her Ambassador's 2002 overtures to NATO by sending Chinese observers to a major NATO submarine escape and rescue exercise (Exercise Sorbet Royal 2002) conducted in the Kattegat, Denmark, from May 20-31, 2002.[59] According to press releases, this exercise involved more than "500 officers, sailors and civilians and 13 surface ships, 4 submarines, and 2 helicopters" with an aim of fostering and improving the "spirit of cooperation in the field of submarine escape and rescue (SMER) and to enhance the interoperability of the participating nations."[60] Notably, there were 79 "visitors and observers" including those from non-NATO nations[61] – and for the first time, China was one of those responding affirmatively to the invitation to send personnel to watch the exercise. The timing of this was significant, in that it occurred after the highly publicized August 2000 Kursk submarine tragedy, and the PLA may have deemed it prudent to gather some techniques and procedures to assess its own capabilities in submarine rescue.

The Chinese did not follow-up to their observation of this exercise with participation in Sorbet Royal 2005, despite a NATO invitation to do so, and so it is difficult to assess the impact it had, if any, on their perceived usefulness of interaction with the Alliance. Clearly, Beijing did not value the exercise enough to make it a habitual relationship – or perhaps participation just fell victim to the neglect of low prioritization. Another possibility is that China found other venues in which to gain submarine escape and rescue training – such as the Asian Pacific Submarine Conference (June 2009), a regional gathering in Singapore in which the PLAN participated.[62]

In November 2009, military staff from NATO's Maritime Command in Northwood, UK, visited Beijing to attend an international counter-piracy meeting hosted by the Chinese Ministry of Defense – a notable instance of an event hosted by the Chinese defense establishment. The purpose of the meeting was to strengthen the international coordination between navies around the world to protect ships from pirate attacks in the Gulf of Aden and the Somali Basin.[63] Yet these discussions only resulted in vague pronouncements, with no discernable concrete changes to existing patrols and actions of SHADE.

These naval interactions are characterized by their low-level, technical, and above all non-policy nature. This is deliberate on the part of Beijing, who prefers to make international contributions under the umbrella and with the mandate of the United Nations, and often in reaction to specific security threats or events. For example, in late 2009, after Chinese ships experienced several prominent piracy attacks, the PLAN reportedly expressed an interest in rotating the SHADE co-chairmanship among all participating navies so that China could serve a turn in that role.[64] Yet despite favorable responses from the countries involved, including encouragement from the SHADE co-chairs, China never followed-up on this proposal and her leadership offer never materialized. Analysts speculated that the delay was due to disagreement in the Central Military Commission (CMC) over the policy implications of taking this step; others believe that the PLAN struggled with the technical aspects of mission assumption, and did not want these weaknesses exposed.[65]

## ENLARGING THE SCOPE: POTENTIAL FOR MUTUAL INTERESTS

Will Sino-NATO cooperation ever launch, or will it remain stalled, a victim of low priority for both parties, with no compelling impetus to push it forward? The status quo – very limited interaction –

may very well continue in the absence of a gripping reason for both parties to engage further. On NATO's side, obstacles to cooperation include the reluctance of some Alliance members (particularly from Eastern European countries) to pursue engagement further, resulting in a lack of consensus regarding broader and deeper relations with China.[66] In addition, on a practical level, ISAF and response to security crises (such as the recent war in Libya) place the biggest demands on NATO time and attention, leaving few resources available for developing ties with a reluctant Beijing. As a US NATO Policy Analyst working for the Joint Staff said, "NATO is a demand-driven organization, so any relationship will be driven by China. More specific requests would help; the Alliance has little time to address general interests."[67]

From China's perspective, drawbacks to cooperation with NATO are many. Beijing has traditionally preferred to engage in bi-lateral, as opposed to multi-lateral, relationships – and when China does engage multi-laterally, it is predominantly through the United Nations or an Asia-Pacific regional organization. China is a Pacific country that claims no security interests on the European continent, and Beijing views NATO as a regional, rather than a global, organization.[68] China's leaders also firmly eschew alliances as a matter of policy. All of this has led to engagement with NATO not surfacing as a near- or mid-term priority for the Chinese.

Some have expressed frustration with the slow pace of developing any contacts between China and NATO. W. Bruce Weinrod, then Defense Advisor for the US Mission to NATO, wrote in the fall of 2008, "As of now, there is no meaningful interaction between China and NATO."[69] In the near-term, progress on engagement has indeed moved slowly. But any engagement is moving forward from the non-interaction that existed between China and NATO for so long.

In light of the apparent Chinese disinterest and the obstacles to closer ties, why pursue cooperation? From NATO's perspective, there are several key reasons. In an era of shrinking defense budgets, NATO is exploring options for maintaining security at a reduced cost, and this may cause the Alliance to become more proactive in shaping the international environment to maximize the possibility of preventing a situation which may eventually necessitate (costly) NATO intervention. Transparency and communication can decrease the chances for misunderstanding, and increase the odds of a peaceful resolution to differences.

NATO focuses on threats that extend beyond and within the Euro-Atlantic zone; as an institution it is continually developing capabilities to handle issues such as counter-piracy, energy security, counter-proliferation, cyber security, and humanitarian assistance/disaster relief.[70] NATO's Secretary General, Anders Fogh Rasmussen, has continually articulated a desire for NATO to "become a forum for consultation on international security concerns"[71] He wants the Alliance to engage emerging powers, such as Brazil, India, and China,[72] and his speeches seem to indicate that he will prioritize this as a legacy of his tenure. For example, at the 2010 Munich Security Conference, China's Xinhua news service reported that Rasmussen outlined his vision for "a permanent network of consultation and cooperation, with NATO as the hub, in which other important international players, such as China, India, and Russia, could take part and discuss views, concerns, and best practices on security or even joint training and planning."[73] This mirrors the relationship that NATO already has with other regions, such as the Mediterranean Dialogue and the Istanbul Cooperation Initiative.

What exactly would China achieve via cooperating with NATO? Some scholars believe that economic nationalism will serve as the driving force behind Chinese actions in the international arena. Robert Kaplan, for instance, argues that China's need for energy and natural resources to sustain its economic growth drives its strategic policy, as Beijing expands its influence on both the land and the sea around its borders to secure this core national interest.[74] Will this compel China to consider working with NATO to protect and/or secure access? While there are certainly other ways to do this, perhaps partnering with NATO has merit as one pillar of Beijing's strategy. Any comprehensive strategic plan will be multi-pronged, avoiding channelizing itself into one single point of failure. Allowing the dialogue with NATO to grow into something more cooperative, perhaps even an institutionalized partnership, would ensure that China has multiple points of access to protect her economic interests in the international arena.

China's other interests in NATO could range from the strategic – showing the global community evidence of "peaceful development" and a willingness for cooperative security engagement – to more tactical – gaining access to the tactics, techniques, and procedures used by the Alliance and its equipment. On the strategic end, China also stands to benefit from increased access to force projection techniques that NATO executes well; these could benefit China's protection of her increasing expat population, as the globalization of Chinese enterprises now finds growing numbers of Chinese citizens living abroad. Developing these skills also has a practical, and more immediate, benefit: China could put HA/DR, crisis management, and counter-piracy techniques to immediate use, both in the Asia-Pacific region and in the water around the Horn of Africa.

## SOFT POWER DEFENSE OF PUBLIC GOODS

Areas that show the most promise for Sino-NATO cooperation are those that not only appeal to mutual interests, but also rely heavily on the "soft" components of power, which provide both sides with increased political acceptance of the engagement. Hence, there are four areas - crisis management, humanitarian assistance/disaster relief, counter-proliferation, and counter-piracy - that offer the most fruitful areas for expanding the relationship. In these areas, short-term mutual tactical gains can increase the probability for continued interaction, and thus lead to the potential for longer-term engagements.

First, crisis management and emergency planning offers the potential for an exchange of ideas and best practices, as well as joint training/cooperation, in an area that has obvious humanitarian benefits. In fact, China has recently approached NATO to express interest in attending courses related to civil emergency planning, civ-mil cooperation, and crisis management, and the Alliance is considering this request.[75] Acquiring greater proficiency in these areas, particularly with some of the higher-level command and control and logistical force projection skills, can increase the PLA's confidence in engaging in these operations beyond China's borders. This is a capability that the Chinese leadership can then highlight as evidence of the country's commitment to supporting the current international system in a peaceful and positive manner. It also benefits soft power projection, in that it results in an ability to influence and attract others to Beijing's way of thinking, which is valuable for building legitimacy. Including China in crisis management and emergency planning training benefits NATO through the increase of interoperability with a rising power that can assist with the maintenance of stability in the international arena.

Along those lines, the second area of engagement that speaks to the interests of both sides is humanitarian assistance/disaster relief. This is a natural outgrowth of cooperation in crisis management and emergency planning, and integrates many of these national military level skills into more complex multi-national operations. Recently, China has shown interest in developing these capabilities and since 2002 China has contributed in some capacity to HA/DR operations in 14 countries.[76] Also, the December 26, 2004 Indian Ocean tsunami clearly highlighted deficiencies in China's ability to respond to natural disasters, even those which occurred nearby. Beijing took notice, and identified the need to improve China's HA/DR support capacity in the country's 2006 Defense White Paper.[77] If China is to develop into a global power, Beijing ought to have the capability to be the "first-responder" to disasters occurring nearby. As Drew Thompson of the Nixon Center recently noted:

> The People's Liberation Army (PLA) has carefully observed the international response to recent disasters, their positive effect on public opinion and the resulting evolution of military thought. Well versed in responding to domestic disasters, such as annual floods and the recent earthquake in Sichuan Province, the PLA is carefully and cautiously assessing the future potential for international disaster relief and humanitarian assistance missions.[78]

NATO's advanced HA/DR capability, coordinated through the Euro-Atlantic Disaster Response Coordination Center (EADRCC), has provided assistance in response to flooding, earthquakes, forest fires, hurricanes, mudflows, and pandemics since its inception in 1998, and thus possesses many of the capabilities that China seeks to enhance.[79] The humanitarian nature of these capabilities also fall into the realm of unimpeachable relief that seeks to assuage human suffering – a notably altruistic cause that receives international praise, and one that often enhances soft power projection. As such, it has appeal as a relatively "safe" area for Chinese assets, both civilian and military, to engage with NATO.

14

The third area that holds promise for engagement is non-proliferation. China has already participated in non-proliferation discussions with NATO, and NATO expects a delegation from Beijing to attend the upcoming Weapons of Mass Destruction annual conference in June 2011 in Oslo.[80] While China has pursued a policy of non-intervention with regard to sovereign state's internal affairs, Beijing is also concerned about the proliferation of nuclear weapons technology, particularly among her neighbors. Although Chinese policy here has been uneven, with Beijing providing sensitive "dual-use" technologies as a tool for gaining access to energy resources, the Chinese do publically state their support of nonproliferation and have privately worked to assist with this, particularly with regard to North Korea.[81]

The fourth and final promising area for engagement is counter-piracy. China's unprecedented involvement in the Gulf of Aden counter-piracy patrols provides solid evidence that this international issue matters to Beijing, and that the government is willing to devote resources toward a solution. Whether this translates into a willingness to cooperate with NATO – as opposed to the United Nations - to ensure free maritime passage of vessels is another matter. On the positive side, the Chinese have provided NATO with a staff-level briefing on their views and role in counter-piracy, marking a key step in sharing information with the Alliance.[82] The fact that the Chinese showed interest in offering this to NATO may be a sign of another incremental step forward in the engagement process. Developing sufficient military capacity to counter maritime attacks would also provide Beijing with another option for dealing with piracy. As a Chinese graduate student articulated, ordinary Chinese citizens currently accept their government using money to counter piracy instead of military force, providing bribes in exchange for security. He noted that China pays to buy back hijacked ships, because Beijing does not have military power; China needs help from others. But, he said, "If we have this military capacity, we would use it. Now, we use money to buy time."[83]

Progress in all areas, while measureable, has been slow. The Chinese have chosen to take a positive view of developments, highlighting the fact that there is, in fact, engagement occurring with NATO. For example, Foreign Ministry spokesperson Jiang Yu stated in May 2007 that China "has resumed and carried out several contacts and exchanges with NATO in various levels and forms, including the first political consultation at the division commander level and the first non-proliferation consultation at the division commander level."[84] Indeed, the dialogue has slowly permeated from the staff/working level into the political realm, and moved onto a new level when the NATO Deputy Secretary General, Claudio Bisogniero, made an official trip to China in November 2009. This marked the first time a high-ranking NATO leader had visited Beijing, and the visit made headlines in both China and Europe. In a speech at the China Institute for International Studies, Beijing, the Deputy Secretary General outlined security challenges which "compel nations to work together…Threats such as the ones I have described – international terrorism, proliferation, piracy, the consequences of failed states – do not stop at our borders."[85]

A European source characterized China's approach to a relationship at this stage as "constructive cautiousness."[86] As the Chinese increasingly show signs of becoming comfortable with more involvement on the global scene, Chinese rhetoric has captured this: "constructive participation" may be the new phrase the PRC uses to gain greater international acceptance of its involvement beyond its borders. At least one Chinese academic based in Beijing has offered this term as a reconceptualization of the principle of non-intervention, and some US State Department personnel feel that it effectively captures the essence of China's new approach to international policy.[87]

Of course, NATO is composed of 28 individual member states, and each has its own foreign policy perspectives and national security interests that may affect relations with China. As mentioned earlier, some Alliance members harbor doubts about the benefits of closer cooperation with China, and fear the potential costs that may develop. On the other hand, the United States arguably has much to gain by encouraging China to engage with NATO. Integrating China as a partner of the Alliance provides yet another means of connecting Beijing to another institution in the current global community, which allows China to develop as a responsible stakeholder while also providing a forum for engagement and mutual benefit. Washington has repeatedly tried to bi-laterally engage China in military-to-military relations, and NATO offers yet another opportunity for communication along these lines. Given that NATO seeks conflict prevention, such interaction with the Chinese could reduce tension, and increase stability in a variety of areas around the globe.

## "SMART DEFENSE" AND THE APPEAL OF SOFT POWER

While NATO's core competence and mission remains as a defensive security alliance, many scholars (particularly constructivists) have attributed its post-Cold War persistence to more than cooperation against a mutual threat. The Alliance continues, they argue, due to the value member states place on maintaining the community of common norms, values, and identities.[88] Many of these norms are based on liberal, Kantian ideals, and can employ non-military means for achieving this end. Attracting global partners into this norm-based system through the use of soft power thus has appeal for the Alliance, as it supports the institution's identity. A possible link between providing security and soft power exists in the global commons areas discussed above.

Yet this approach, and the soft power uses it entails, also presents difficulties for NATO. Europeans tend to view the European Union as the purveyor of soft power, while NATO is the military alliance; if these boundaries start to blur, then questions may arise as to the necessity of having two

16

organizations; following this line of thinking leads to the logical conclusion that the transatlantic link is the only differentiating characteristic.

Still, many questions exist regarding Beijing's willingness to utilize NATO as a forum for engagement. Are there Chinese internal divisions over cooperation with NATO? Presumably, all factions within the Chinese regime will not view interaction with NATO equally, and this is an area for further research. What is the view of the PLA toward NATO? This has also not been clear to observers. And yet the positions taken by these domestic elements could drastically affect the shape that any engagement takes.

Some Chinese analysts express skepticism that Beijing will prioritize cooperation with NATO. According to Tao Wenzhao, a professor at the Institute of American Studies of the Chinese Academy of Social Sciences, "NATO has been eyeing deeper ties with China for some time, because they are looking for substantial help from China to ease things up in Afghanistan, a nine-year-old war that has required the deployment of 150,000 multinational troops."[89] Tao cites Beijing's commitment to non-alliance, as well as NATO's Cold War mission, as reasons that China will not deepen a relationship with NATO.

The public might also present some skepticism if Beijing increases ties with NATO. As a Chinese graduate student noted, "Ordinary people in China believe that NATO is a military organization led by the US. People do not have a positive view of US when the focus is on the military. So, we focus on the EU, because it is not military and not US. US-led is the key Chinese sticking point for cooperation with NATO. Ordinary people would be more confident if we can find a global organization without the US, we like it."[90]

But if Chinese policymakers follow this path of thinking, they will miss an opportunity to demonstrate Beijing's willingness to engage the global community when mutual interests coincide, while still remaining true to a "lay low" foreign policy. While NATO may not be the first regional alliance on Chinese priority lists, it offers long-term potential for Beijing in a number of significant areas. And although it is a security alliance, engagement with NATO could provide a politically acceptable launching point for China's foray into the wider global security community.

# ENDNOTES

[1] Quoted in *China Daily*, "NATO Chief Eyes Closer Ties with China, India," 8 February 2010. Accessed 18 February 2011, http://www.chinadaily.com.cn/2010-02/08/content_9442882.htm

[2] See, for example, Joshua Kurlantzick, *Charm Offensive: How China's Soft Power is Transforming the World* (Yale University Press, New Haven and London: 2007) and Joseph Nye, Jr., "The Rise of China's Soft Power," *The Wall Street Journal Asia*, op-ed, December 29. 2007.

[3] "Strategic Concept for the Defence and Security of the Members of the North Atlantic Treaty Organisation", Adopted by Heads of State and Government in Lisbon: Active Engagement, Modern Defence. 19 November 2010. Accessed 18 February 2011, http://www.nato.int/strategic-concept/index.html.

[4] See Joseph Nye, Jr., *Soft Power: The Means to Success in World Politics*, Public Affairs, 2004, 5.

[5] Per Magnus Wijkman, "Managing the Global Commons," *International Organization* 36,3, Summer 1982:511.

[6] For a complete listing of forces provided to ISAF by non-member nations, see International Security Force Afghanistan, "Troop Numbers and Contributions," (ISAF Placemat), 4 March 2011, accessed 7 March 2011, http://www.isaf.nato.int/troop-numbers-and-contributions/index.php

[7] See, for example, Jonathan S. Landay, "China's Thirst for Copper Could Hold Key to Afghanistan's Future," McClatchy Newspapers, 8 March 2009, accessed 13 January 2011, http://www.mcclatchydc.com/2009/03/08/63452/chinas-thirst-for-copper-could.html

[8] "NATO Chief Eyes Closer Ties with China, India," *China Daily*, 8 February 2010, accessed 23 January 2011, http://www.chinadaily.com.cn/2010-02/08/content_9442882.htm

[9] European source, telephonic interview with author, 23 February 2011.

[10] See the Ministry of the Foreign Affairs of the People's Republic of China, "Conclusion of the 'Sino-Soviet Treaty of Friendship, Alliance and Mutual Assistance," accessed 18 February 2011, http://www.fmprc.gov.cn/eng/ziliao/3602/3604/t18011.htm

[11] Peter Calvocoressi, *Survey of International Affairs*, 1949-1950, Oxford University Press, 1953, London, p340, cited in Xiyu Chen, "From Political Alliance in China's Conception to Comprehensive Partnership in Building: the Relations between China and the European Community/European Union", Dissertation zur Erlangung des akademischen Grades Doktor der Sozialwissenschaften in der Fakultät für Sozial- und Verhaltenswissenschaften der Eberhard-Karls-Universität Tübingen, 2003: 18.

[12] See Xiyu, 18, and June Teufel Dryer, *China's Political System: Modernization and Tradition*, 8th ed. Longman, an imprint of Pearson: New York, 2012: 336-337.

[13] Mao's exact words came from a speech delivered "In Commemoration of the Twenty-eighth Anniversary of the Communist Party of China", available from the Selected Works of Mao Tse-tung at http://www.wellesley.edu/Polisci/wj/China/mao22.html : "You are leaning to one side." Exactly. The forty years' experience of Sun Yat-sen and the twenty-eight years' experience of the Communist Party have taught us to lean to one side, and we are firmly convinced that in order to win victory and consolidate it we must lean to one side. In the light of the experiences accumulated in these forty years and these twenty-eight years, all Chinese without exception must lean either to the side of imperialism or to the side of socialism. Sitting on the fence will not do, nor is there a third road. See also Hao Yufan and Zhai Zhihai, "China's Decision to Enter the Korean War: History Revisited", The China Quarterly. No. 121 (March 1990): 97.

[14] Pan Zhenqiang, "China and NATO in the Future", Foreign Affairs Journal, No. 75, Academy of International Studies and Department of International Relations, Nankai University, accessed 18 February 2011, http://irchina.org/en/xueren/china/view.asp?id=817

[15] Xinghui Zhang, "NATO Needs to Think Twice about its Future", *NATO Review* http://www.nato.int/docu/review/2008/08/FUTURE_OF_NATO/EN/index.htm

[16] See United States Forces Korea, "United Nations Command", accessed 21 February 2011, http://www.usfk.mil/usfk/content.united_nations.command.68

[17] David C. Isby & Charles Kamps Jr, *Armies of NATO's Central Front*, Jane's Publishing Company Ltd 1985, p.13-14.

[18] See North Atlantic Treaty Organization, "NATO's Strategic Documents Since 1949," accessed 26 February 2011. http://www.nato.int/cps/en/natolive/topics_56626.htm

[19] For a thorough discussion of NATO's reaction to the Korean War, see Lawrence S. Kaplan, *NATO Divided, NATO United: The Evolution of an Alliance.* Westport, CT: Praeger, 2004.

[20] Quote cited in Arthur Waldron, "Nixon and Taiwan in 1972: The Week that Didn't Change the World" in *The "One China" Dilemma*, edited by Peter C. Y. Chow. Palgrave MacMillan, New York: 2008: 166.

[21] Quote cited in Evelyn Goh, "Nixon, Kissinger, and the 'Soviet Card' in the U.S. Opening to China, 1971-1974" Diplomatic History, Vol. 29, No. 3 (June 2005): 487.

[22] Zhou-Ye Jianying-Kissinger memcon, 20/6/72, pp. 15–6; 6/21/72, p.3, in Box 851, National Security Files (NSF), Nixon Presidential Material (NPM), National Archives (NA), cited in Goh, 485.

[23] Mao-Kissinger memcon, 2/17/73, in Burr, *Kissinger Transcripts*, 88–89, cited in Goh, 485.

[24] David Shambaugh, "China Eyes Europe's Role in the World: Real Convergence or Cognitive Dissonance?," in David Shambaugh, et. al., *China-Europe Relations*. (Taylor & Francis, Inc.: 2007) :139.

Ding Yuanhong, "The European Situation in Flux, " p30.

[25] People's Daily, "Backgrounder: Basic Facts About NATO", November 19, 2010. Accessed 17 February 2011, http://english.people.com.cn/90001/90777/90856/7205270.html

[26] European Union External Action, "China" Accessed 28 February 2011, http://eeas.europa.eu/china/index_en.htm

[27] See Europa Press Release, "EU-China Summit (Brussels, 6 October 2010), MEMO/10/462, dated 30 September 2010, accessed 4 March 2011: http://europa.eu/rapid/pressReleasesAction.do?reference=MEMO/10/462 "Since bilateral ties between the EU and China were established thirty five years ago, trade relations have expanded from €4 billion in 1978 to €296 billion in 2009. Today, the EU is China's most important trading partner, while for the EU, China is second only to the United States."

[28] Stockholm International Peace Research Institute, "Council of Ministers Declaration on China," European Council: Madrid, 26-27 June 1989. Accessed 14 January 2011, http://www.sipri.org/research/armaments/transfers/controlling/arms_embargoes/eu_arms_embargoes/china/declaration

[29] Ibid.

[30] See Kerry Dumbaugh, "Chinese Embassy Bombing in Belgrade: Compensation Issues," CRS Report for Congress, accessed 17 February 2011, http://congressionalresearch.com/RS20547/document.php

[31] Elizabeth Rosenthal, "Crisis in the Balkans: China; More Anti-U.S. Protests in Beijing as Officials Study Bombing Error,"10 May 1999. Accessed 4 March 2011 at http://www.nytimes.com/1999/05/10/world/crisis-balkans-china-more-anti-us-protests-beijing-officials-study-bombing-error.html?ref=jamesrsasser

[32] See Ministry of Foreign Affairs of the People's Republic of China, "Strong Protest by the Chinese Government Against the Bombing by the US-led NATO of the Chinese Embassy in the Federal Yugoslavia," 17 November 2000. Accessed 26 February 2011: http://www.fmprc.gov.cn/eng/ziliao/3602/3604/t18047.htm

[33] Ibid.

[34] "10th Anniversary of the Bombing of the Chinese Embassy in Belgrade," *People's Daily Online*, 9 May 2009. Accessed 18 February 2011. http://english.peopledaily.com.cn/90001/90776/6654193.html

[35] Yao Ning, interview with author, Ash Center, Harvard University, 4 February 2011.

[36] Yao Yao, interview with author, Ash Center, Harvard University, 4 February 2011.

[37] European source, telephonic interview with author, 23 February 2011.

[38] David Helvey, Principal Director for East Asia, interview with author, Washington, D.C., 9 February 2011.

[39] North Atlantic Treaty Organization online, "NATO's Role in Afghanistan," last updated 4 February 2011, Accessed 18 February 2011. http://www.nato.int/cps/en/natolive/topics_8189.htm

[40] Reyko Huang, "Fact Sheet: International Security Assistance Force (ISAF) in Afghanistan," Center for Defense Information, updated 14 February 2002. Accessed 18 February 2011. http://www.cdi.org/terrorism/isaf.cfm

[41] U.S. Department of State, *Patterns of Global Terrorism 2001*, May 21, 2002: 16.

[42] "Chinese President Expressed Sympathy to Bush, U.S. Government and People for Disastrous Attacks," *People's Daily* online, 12 September 2001.

[43] J. Mohan Malik, "Dragon on Terrorism: Assessing China's Tactical Gains and Strategic Losses After 11 September," *Contemporary Southeast Asia*, Vol. 24, No. 2, August 2002: 260.

[44] U.S. Department of State, *Patterns of Global Terrorism 2001*, May 21, 2002: 16-17.

[45] See Holly Fletcher, "Backgrounder: The East Turkestan Islamic Movement (ETIM)" Council on foreign Relations, July 31, 2008. Available at: http://www.cfr.org/china/east-turkestan-islamic-movement-etim/p9179 The Eastern Turkistan Islamic Movement (ETIM) is also known as the East Turkistan Islamic Party (ETIP); see United States Department of State, *2009 Country Reports on Terrorism - China*, 5 August 2010, available at: http://www.unhcr.org/refworld/docid/4c63b64fa.html

[46] See Dennis Roy, "Lukewarm Partner: Chinese Support for U.S. Counter-Terrorism in Southeast Asia,"

Asia-Pacific Center for Security Studies, March 2006.

[47] Zuqian Zhang, "Beijing Calling," *NATO Review*, Autumn 2003. Accessed 19 February 2011, http://www.nato.int/docu/review/2003/issue3/english/special.html

[48] Ibid.

[49] European source, telephonic interview with author, 23 February 2011.

[50] For a discussion on the Sino-Pakistan relationship, see Andrew Small, "China's Af-Pak Moment," Policy Brief, Asia Program, The German Marshal Fund of the United States, 20 May 2009. See also Michael D. Swaine, "China and the 'AfPak' Issue," *China Leadership Monitor*, No. 31.

[51] See Anne Applebaum, "China's Quiet Power Grab," op-ed, *The Washington Post*, 28 September 2010. Accessed 4 November 2010. http://www.washingtonpost.com/wp-dyn/content/article/2010/09/27/AR2010092704658.html

[52] See Swaine, 8 and Nirav Patel and David Capezza. "From Washington to Kabul to Beijing: Assessing Prospects for U.S.-China-Afghanistan Cooperation" *Small Wars Journal*. April 1, 2009,

available at http://smallwarsjournal.com/blog/journal/docs-temp/206-patel.pdf.

[53] Richard Weitz, "The Limits of Partnership: China, NATO and the Afghan War." *China Security*, Vol. 6 No. 1, 2010: 21-35.

[54] Roger Cliff, "Anti-Access Measures in Chinese Defense Strategy", Testimony presented before the US China Economic and Security Review Commission on January 27, 2011.

[55] Small, "China's 'Af-Pak' Moment".

[56] David Helvey, Principal Director for East Asia, interview with author, Washington, D.C., 9 February 2011.

[57] European source, telephonic interview with author, 23 February 2011.

[58] See "China to lead SHADE's anti-piracy patrols off Somalia" in China Defense Blog, 28 January 2010, available at http://china-defense.blogspot.com/2010/01/china-to-lead-shades-anti-piracy.html. SHADE began in 2008 to coordinate activities between the countries and organizations involved in military counter-piracy operations in international waters surrounding Somalia. Members use monthly coordination meetings, held in Bahrain, to discuss practical measures for ensuring coverage of the maritime space. See Lisa M. Novak, "Naval Officials Discuss Anti-

Piracy Tactics," European Stars and Stripes, 28 May 2009.  Available at http://www.stripes.com/news/naval-officials-discuss-anti-piracy-tactics-1.92060

[59] "Sorbet Royal 2002" Initial Press Release, RHQ Eastlant/HQ Navnorth, NATO, available at: http://www.sorbetroyal2002.celex.net/press_info/iepr_htm, and European source, telephonic interview with author, 23 February 2011.

[60] "Sorbet Royal 2002" Initial Press Release and  Commander David M. Osen, USNR, "Exercise Sorbet Royal 2002 Tests Navy's Deep Submergence Unit's Submarine Rescue Capabilities" RHQ Eastlant/HQ Navnorth, NATO, available at: http://www.sorbetroyal2002.celex_net/press_info/30_may_2002_(4).htm

[61] Ibid.

[62] According to the International Submarine Escape and Rescue Liaison Office, who reported on the conference, "The People's Liberation Army Navy system, LR-7, has been delivered by Perry Slingsby System in the late 2008. It has now completed a deep-dive trial to more than 500 meters and conducted matings with PLA Navy submarines. It is now rescue ready and Chinese rescue team is looking forward for further training." Accessed 4 March 2011. http://www.ismerlo.org/

[63] NATO Newsroom, "NATO Military Visits Beijing to Discuss Piracy Operations," 11 November 2009.  Available at: http://www.nato.int/cps/en/natolive/news_59000_htm

[64] Richard Weitz, "Priorities and Challenges in China's Naval Deployment in the Horn of Africa" China Brief Vol 9 Issue 24, 3 December 2009.  Available at: http://www.jamestown.org/programs/chinabrief/single/?tx_ttnews%5Btt_news%5D=35795&tx_ttnews%5BbackPid%5D=25&cHash=8c7b43d6ae

[65] Greg Torode, "PLA Delays Taking Lead on Piracy", South China Morning Post, 21 June 2010, pg.1.

[66] Mark Foster, Deputy, NATO Policy Division, J-5, The Joint Staff, interview with author, Washington, D.C., 9 February 2011.

[67] Mark Foster, Deputy, NATO Policy Division, J-5, The Joint Staff, interview with author, Washington, D.C., 9 February 2011.

[68] Chen Zheng, interview with author, Ash Center, Harvard University, 4 February 2011.  Yao Yao, interview with author, Ash Center, Harvard University, 4 February 2011.

[69] W. Bruce Weinrod, "NATO and Asia's Changing Relationship", Global Asia, Vol 3 No3 Fall 2008.

[70] Mark Foster, Deputy, NATO Policy Division, J-5, The Joint Staff, interview with author, Washington, D.C., 9 February 2011.

[71] NATO Secretary General 26 JAN 11 video blog

[72] European source, telephonic interview with author, 23 February 2011.

[73] "NATO Chief Eyes Closer Ties with China, India," China Daily, 8 February 2010.  Accessed 18 February 2011, http://www.chinadaily.com.cn/2010-02/08/content_9442882.htmhttp://www.chinadaily.com.cn/2010-02/08/content_9442882_htm

[74] Robert D. Kaplan, "The Geography of Chinese Power" Foreign Affairs, May/June 2010:  22.

[75] Mark Foster, Deputy, NATO Policy Division, J-5, The Joint Staff, interview with author, Washington, D.C., 9 February 2011.

[76] Ian Storey, "Hospital Ships Can Be China's 'Diplomats'" The Straits Times, April 8, 2009. http://www.iseas.edu.sg/viewpoint/is8apr09.pdf

[77] Ibid.

[78] Drew Thompson, "International Disaster Relief and Humanitarian Assistance:  A Future Role for the PLA?" China Brief, Vol. 8 Issue 11 (June 6, 2008) Available online at:

http://www.jamestown.org/programs/chinabrief/single/?tx_ttnews%5Btt_news%5D=4941&tx_ttnews%5BbackPid%5D=168&no_cache=1

[79] See Euro-Atlantic Disaster Response Coordination Centre (EADRCC), accessed 4 March 2011. http://www.nato.int/eadrcc/

[80] European source, telephonic interview with author, 23 February 2011.

[81] See Richard Weitz, "Understanding China's Evolving Role in Global Security Challenges," in Abraham Denmark and Nirav Patel, eds., *China's Arrival: A Strategic Framework for a Global Relationship*, (Washington, D.C.: Center for a New American Security: 2009): 81-85.

[82] European source, telephonic interview with author, 23 February 2011.

[83] Yao Ning, interview with author, Ash Center, Harvard University, 4 February 2011.

[84] "China Willing to Strengthen Ties with NATO" Xinhua, 25 May 2007, available at: http://www.chinadaily.com.cn/china/2007-05/25/content_880191.htm

[85] Speech by NATO Deputy Secretary General Claudio Bisogniero at the China Institute for International Studies, Beijing, China, 10 November 2009. Available at:

http://www.nato.int/cps/en/SID-23B759E7-DC519596/natolive/opinions_59185_htm?selectedLocale=en

[86] European source, telephonic interview with author, 23 February 2011.

[87] Phrase used by an academic from the Peking University School of International Studies. State Department sentiments expressed during interviews with the author, 1 May 2009, Beijing.

[88] See Helene Sjursen, "On the Identity of NATO" *International Affairs* 80, 4 (2004): 687-703.

[89] Bao Daozu, "NATO Alliance Seeks to Engage China", *China Daily Online*, 15 October 2010. Available at: http://www.chinadaily.com.cn/china/2010-10/15/content_11413319.htm

[90] Yao Ning, interview with author, Ash Center, Harvard University, 4 February 2011.